Mrs. Merryman's Collection

Mrs. Merryman's Collection

Presented by Anne Sophie Merryman

About my grandmother's collection

My grandmother, Anne-Marie Merryman, was born in 1920 in London and died in 1980, the year I was born. Although I don't have any memories of meeting her, I inherited two things from her: my first name and a small wooden box. Inside the box were old postcards, which she had collected throughout her life. I've heard that she rarely travelled outside England and didn't receive these postcards herself but that she collected them for the images and used to look at them for hours whilst seated in her armchair.

When I was growing up, my favourite thing to do was to look at the postcards and imagine my grandmother's life, her character and her intimate thoughts. Time has left its marks on their surfaces and each image took me to a different and unknown world.

The delight of being in the realms of the imagination encouraged my growing fascination with storytelling and fiction, and probably led me to pursue a career in acting.

I still don't know who my grandmother really was, but through her collection I feel that I can have a personal dialogue with her, even if that is only my fantasy.

Anne Sophie Merryman

RAG. MASS.ᴺᴼ DEL MAGRO

LIVORNO

*

RAPPRESENTANTE

Drucksache

Sig. Giuseppe Giunti
fuori porta Elisa
Lucca

FABBRI & C. – LIVORNO 62

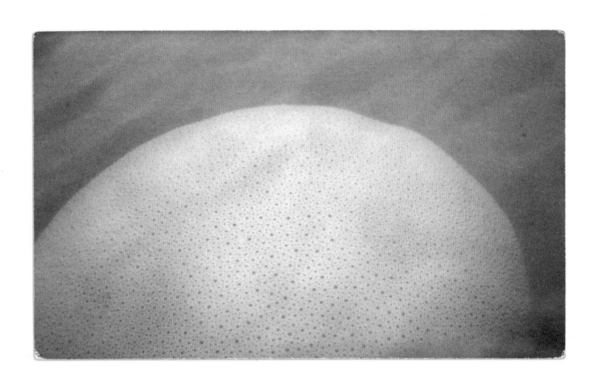

POSTKARTE.
CARTE POSTALE-CARTOLINA POSTALE.
POST CARD

M

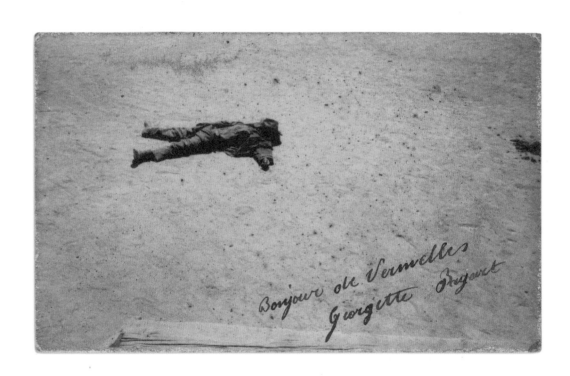

Bonjour de Vermelles
Georgette Bugeaud

Lille le 4

Deux mots ...

M. et Mme
Courchelle Luglien
Maréchal à
Vermeilles
Pas de Calais

Postkarte.

Tuesday

Received your P.C. to-day.
Auntie L. has gone to Mrs Williams.
Mr & H. has been to Sheffield.
Mrs H. not looking quite so
well, but Dr says as well
as can be expected.

Had a card for you.
from Burton this morning
Have not heard from Miss
M. yet.

Love
Alfred

P.S. Did well Monday — 6-30.

Mrs H. N. Biggin

24 Leighton Rd

Moseley

Birmingham

Bs Olives a 1 Décembre 1904   La famille Duchez de Bs Olives adresse à

à ses chers Parents de Lyon ses affectueuses salutations et meilleurs souhaits
à l'occasion du nouvel an en attendant qu'elle leur écrive

TARJETA POSTAL

Correspondencia   Dirección

Amigo mio:

No he recibido has-
ta hoy carta de Ud.
¿Se habrá extravia-
do su corresponden-
cia?
Dígame Ud. siquiera
que "sí". J. Soto.

Callao, Julio 24/913.

Señor
Julio Peñaylillo,
Vista de la Aduana de
Oruro.
Bolivia.

Sanmartí y Ca. 5585

7. Le Môle

PRIVATE POST CARD

THIS SPACE MAY BE USED FOR CORRESPONDENCE

THIS SPACE IS FOR ADDRESS ONLY.

Bonjour
Bons baisers
ta mère Aline

Mademoiselle
Jacqueline Courchelle
Rue Jules Guesde
Vermelles
(P.D.C)

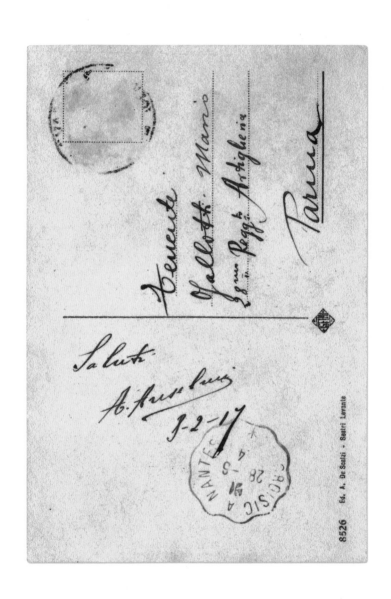

Tenente
Gallotti. Mario
28.m Regg.t Artiglieria

Parma

Saluti
A. Anselmi
1-2-17

8526   Ed. A. De Scalzi - Scatri Levante

NANTES A
BORDISIC A
28
4-5
17

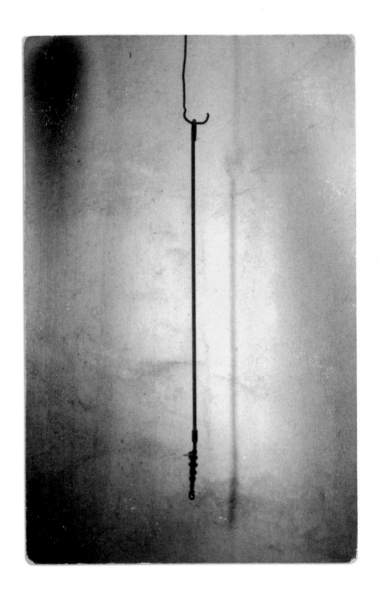

BILHETE POSTAL

Union Postale Universelle

Direcção

Correspondencia

3369-t. Meknes. Medicine Man.

Pola. 1915.

Such a lovely place right on
the sea with Roman ruins.
loving it. K.

UNION POSTAL UNIVERSAL
UNION POSTALE UNIVERSELLE
ESPAÑA

A Sig. Pirrello Egidio

Calosso - Asti

(Provincia - Alessandria)

Italia

POST *Fry's* CARD

PREMIER JOUR D'ÉMISSION
HISTORIQUE   F.D.C.

Tarjeta Postal
Union postal universal

Carte po poste italiane

Postkarte

4 X 19
1958

Señor
Julio Lenaydillo
y familia
La Paz
Bolivia

Villa Bella, 30./11 /15.

Querido Julio:
Por la pte. te deseo
à ti y tu familia
todo genero de felici-
dades en el nuevo
año.   Tu fiel amigo
Karl

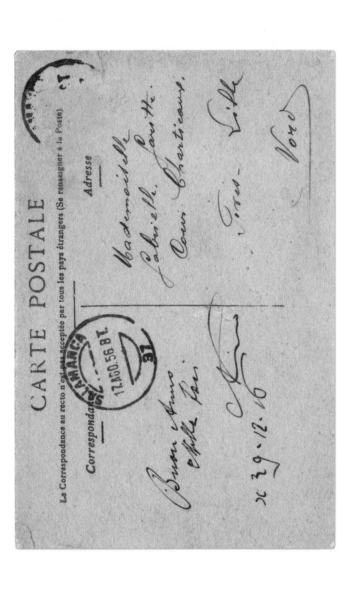

CARTE POSTALE

La Correspondance au recto n'est pas acceptée par tous les pays étrangers (Se renseigner à la Poste)

Correspondance

Adresse

Mademoiselle
Gabrielle Lanotte
Cour Chartreaux.

Lille
sous-

Nord

Bon Anno
e Felle Jour

x 29·12·16

136. BAC HA -- Panorama de la Ville

KÖLN · DOM
Ab 1248 in 623 Jahren erbaut.
Höhe der Türme: 157 m

Hans Andres Verlag, Hamburg — Photo: Hans Hartz

Echte
Fotografie
K 131/2030

Blankenberghe   Marée haute.

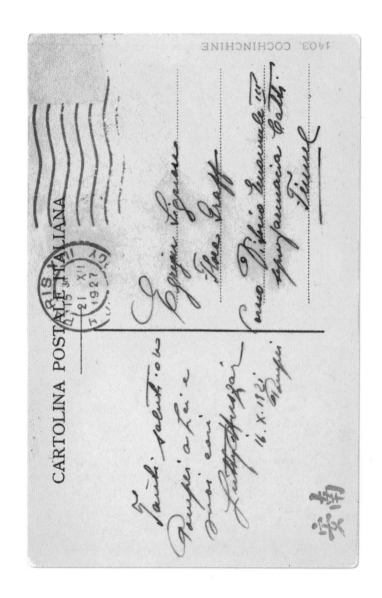

CARTOLINA POSTALE ITALIANA

1403. COCHINCHINE

Egregia Signora
Sara Graff
Corso Vittorio Emanuele III
Spnjaoucia Catt.
Fiume

Tanti saluti
auguri affre
dai vostri
Luttifappufar
16.X.1927
Bruges

El Ajuste.

(Cuento muy breve)

En mi tierra hay la costumbre,
entre gentes de lugar,
de dotar a las mujeres
cuando se van a casar.
Refieren, que, muchas veces,
por un burro o un collar,
desbaratan el ajuste,
y de boda no hay que hablar.
Trae un garrido mozo,
de posición regular,
que quería a su zagala
con afecto singular.
De ambas partes se juntaron
las familias a ajustar,
mil detalles y otros más.
La zagala era ambiciosa
y mimada por demás,
y a más de otros regalitos
antojósele un collar
de oro, aljófar y coral.
El mozo, que no tenía
en la mano, tal caudal,

negóse a lo del collar,
prometiendo, con el tiempo,
el regalo presentar.
Y, después de estar casado
é instalados en su hogar,
pues pensaba, para entonces,
reunir más capital.

(Sigue al nº 2)

Srta. Luisa de la Revilla y

de la Fuente

Refitolería 5

Segovia

Auteuil le 21. 12. 30

Chère Madame

Vous savez que je n'ai
pas de "jours" réguliers
mais je serai à la
maison dimanche
prochain 28 décembre
pour quelques intimes.
Voulez-vous venir
aussi afin que je
ne puisse pas l'année
dans la solitude ?
Il est superflu de
vous dire que vos

Mme Lambert
9 rue Charlot

Paris

CARTE POSTALE

CM

ADRESSE

Mlle Madeleine Sai...

N° 108 Avenue Ledru Rollin

Paris.

Seine

le 9 Décembre 1916.

Bon Souvenir.

Ton Cousin qui t'embrasse

Geoffroi

83 — J. PEU   Cementerio de Indios Patagones

I - HELSINKI (Finlande)

PAINOTUOTE
(IMPRIMÉ)

ANTIBIOTICOS, S. A. - Castellana, 8 - MADRID

POST CARD

Wildt & Kray, London E. C. Series 731.

WIEDEMANN'S KÜNSTLERKARTE.

Verlag der Saalburgverwaltung.

KÜNSTLER-SERIE "WIRO" SAALBURG II. No. 2005 A.
C. F. Wiedemann, Hofl., Roda S.-A.
Ges. geschützt.

Bonne fête
Vive Sainte Catherine

BUONA
PASQUA

Augustin et Constance   Noeux le 25 novbre 1909

Carte Postale
Postkarte — Post card
Cartolina Postale — Levelezö-lap
Bréfkort — Briefkaart — Brevkort
ОТКРЫТОЕ ПИСЬМО
Tarjeta postal — Carto postal
Union postale universelle
Dopisnice

Mademoiselle Aline Caillières

Couturière à Verquigneul

Par Béthune

Cordoba - 18-6-1920

Tanti baci a voi
e a mamma da
papà che vi
ricorda sempre —
Saluti affettuosi a [illegible]

TALLERES ARGENTINOS PEUSER

CARTE POSTALE

(TARJETA POSTAL)

UNION POSTALE UNIVERSELLE

EDITION LA PAGODE SOE

31. - Grande Dame annamite

Signori

Enrico e Olga Lunario

Gascon - 3154 -

Buenos Aires

Reservado para la dirección.

402 - Basajaun.

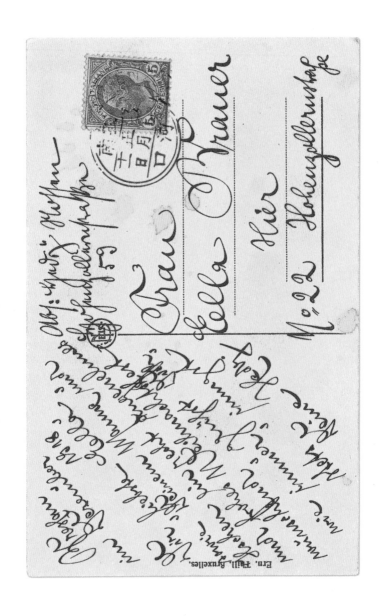

Frau

Hella Brauer

Hier

No 22 Hohenzollerndaf

POST CARD.

This space may be used for communication
between Great Britain, the Colonies, and
some Foreign Countries.

The Address only to be written here.

Printed at the works in Berlin

28 356   Photo Tourists Association.   Turnham Green W.

Dear Lucy
Just a line to out
wish you many happy
returns will get you
something when I
get back with love

W.A.B

Miss L. Prior,
107 Haydons P.R. Rd,
Wimbledon.

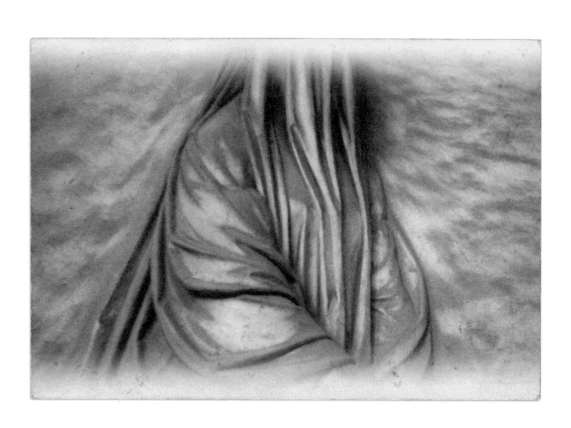

Querida amiga Paula:

Siendo mañana
el día de tu fiesta
onomástica le envío
la felicitación más
sincera y cariñosa
tu amiga que la
quiere y no la ol-
vida Pepita

Srta
Paula de la Re-
villa
Madrid

Eibar 28-6-935

Edit. La Cigogne, 32, rue Porte-dijeaux - Bordeaux

A 762   Un crepúsculo en el río Cruz del Eje — Rep. Argentina

Miss Alice H Moseley

Bradda, Port Erin

Isle of Man

England

BUENOS AIRFS
NC 21
17
1929

Zürich 26. XII. 1912
zeltweg 65

With all best wishes
for a happy New Year
from Hermine Geisler

Carte Postale

POST CARD — POSTKARTE — CARTOLINA POSTALE
TARJETA POSTAL

Correspondance

Adresse

SITGES. -61   Atardecer

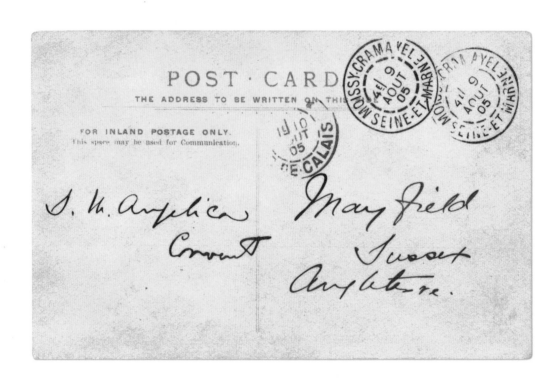

POST · CARD

THE ADDRESS TO BE WRITTEN ON THIS [...]

FOR INLAND POSTAGE ONLY.
This space may be used for Communication.

S. M. Angelica
Cronant

Mary field

Sussex

Angleterre.

COLLECTION PETIT JOURNAL

UNION POSTALE UNIVERSELLE

PORTUGAL

BILHETE POSTAL — CARTE POSTALE

Texto — Texte

Endereço — Adresse

TABACARIA INGLEZA

Souvenir du Marché

Bonne Année

C. Maegerman

Mademoiselle jacqueline
bourchille

au Pensionnat Notre dame

La Bassée

Nord,

Chocolat GARDON - Cambrai

Pozdrowienia z pięknej okolicy
Wujcia Zolja'u rasydey's Mysia i Tw

Carte postale.

Postkarte. Cartolina postale.

COTE réservé à l'adresse. FRANKSEITE
Francostature siehe RÜCKSEITE

Famille Chevallier

5. villa acacias

Conflans-St-honorine

(S.k.o)

France

Djibouti 9/12/06

MONTREUX 23.VI.11.-5

Liebe Mutter

Besten Gruss
sendet ihre
lieber Sohn

Der Jacob

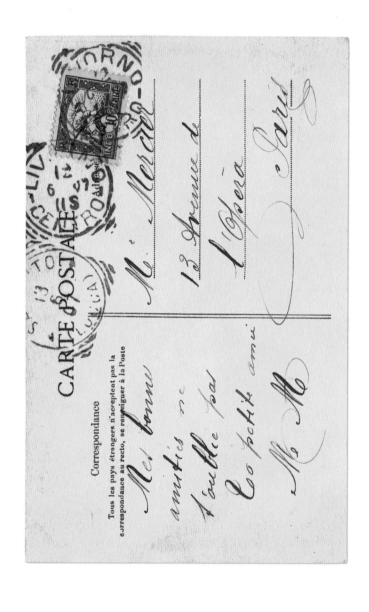

CARTE POSTALE

Correspondance

Tous les pays étrangers n'acceptent pas la
correspondance au recto, se renseigner à la Poste

Mes bonnes
amitiés ne
m'oublie pas
ton petit ami

Mo Mo

M. Mercier
13 Avenue de
l'Opéra
Paris

Hinterzarten

Titisee, 885m ü. M., mit Feldberg und Hinterzarten

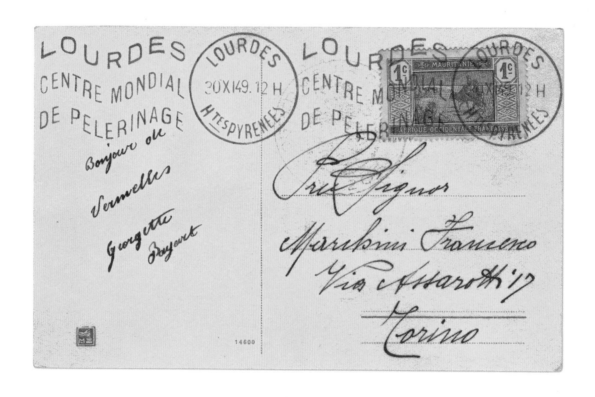

LOURDES
CENTRE MONDIAL
DE PELERINAGE

LOURDES
30 XI 49. 12 H
H.TES PYRENEES

LOURDES
CENTRE MONDIAL
DE PELER

Bonjour ou

Vermelles

Georgette
Boyart

Pour Signor

Marchini Francesco
Via Assarotti 17

Torino

14600

KIKIMORA

Wyd. Polskiego Towarzystwa Księgarni Kolejowych „RUCH"
Przedruk wzbroniony

ROOSENDAAL
16 VI 9
1958

Marys myję kochana!
Pred chwilą wróciłem. ze
Stanisławem do Lwowa. Jeszcze
się nie rozstaję drobolym,
być może Przemyśl. Wróć
idzy się w poniedziałek znow
Lekka zupełnie zdrów i nie
zmęczony. Teraz wygodnie
w dzień. Uwas ni Lylko
wiadomości od Was. Wczoraj
wieczór spędziłem z Himeć. Dziś
zdaje się Hdy musi et to samo
zrobić, bo nie wiem gdzie się
podział. Zatem słysba wylicz
się ciereem do
Esteciew. Ucałowuję Was bardo
serdecznie Jacek   Czwartek 12/
Lwów.   XI 25

Wielmożna
Marja Piotrowska
Warszawa
Smolna 32,1.

POST CARD.

The Morland Series.

COMMUNICATION

Je vous donne de mes nouvelles
Je me porte très
bien je pense que
vous vous portez bien
aussi amitiés

[illegible]

ADDRES

Mr Mary
Bd de la Roquette
166
Paris

Nº 2402   Souq.   Published by Soe&co., Azrou

POST-CARD

COURONNE DU BLASON
MÉD TERRANÉE

Serie 650

Edit. The Cairo Post-Card Trust - Ph. N. 051

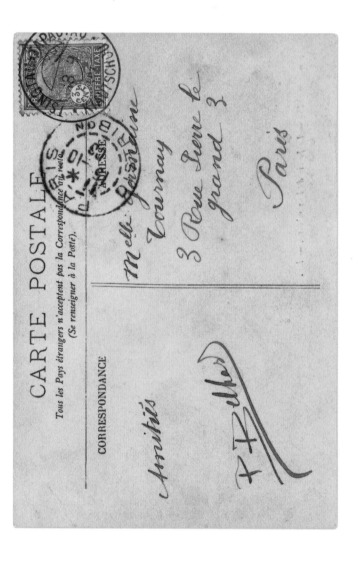

CARTE POSTALE

Tous les Pays étrangers n'acceptent pas la Correspondance au verso.
(Se renseigner à la Poste).

CORRESPONDANCE

Amitiés

M elle Joséphine
Tournay
3 Rue Pierre le
grand 3
Paris

CARTE POSTALE

Ce côté est exclusivement réservé à l'adresse

M. Seyn Hodgkinson
10, Portland St
Leamington Spa

Établissements Photographiques de NEURDEIN Frères. — Paris

A young Zau girl

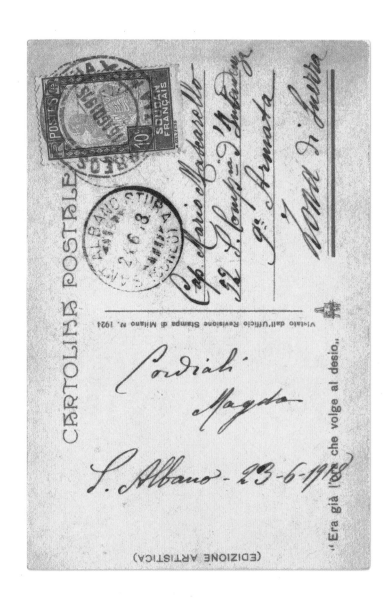

CARTOLINA POSTALE

Vietato dall'Ufficio Revisione Stampa di Milano N. 1924

(EDIZIONE ARTISTICA)

Cap. Mario Albarello
92 L'Bonifica d'Intendenza
9ª Armata
Zona di Guerra

Cordiali
Magda

S. Albano - 23-6-1918

"Era già l'ora che volge al desio,,

POST CARD.

"Dainty" Series.

The Address to be written here

This Space may be used for Correspondence.

PRINTED-IN-ENGLAND.

6296

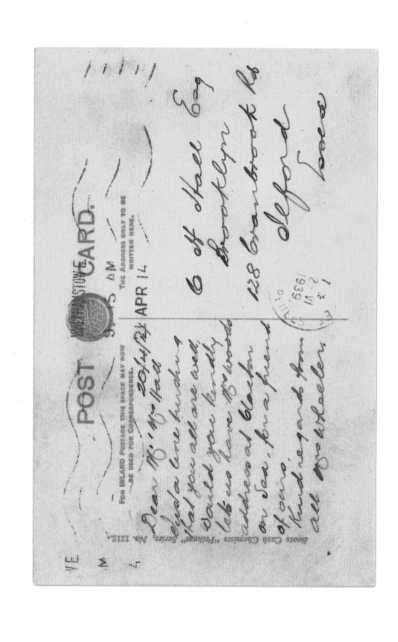

POST CARD.

FELIXSTOWE
9.15 AM
APR 14

20/4/14

Dear Mr. Mollatt
I just drop a line wishing
that you all are well,
would you kindly
let me have the woods
address of Electon
on Sea. for a friend
of ours.
Kind regards to
all Mr. Wheeler.

6 St Kael Esq
Brooklyn
128 Cranbrook Rd
Ilford
Essex

Post card

ОТКРЫТОЕ ПИСЬМО

VISITE SITGES
EXPOSICION NACIONAL
DE CLAVELES
PLAYA DE ORO

First edition published by MACK

Mrs. Merryman's Collection is the winner of the First Book Award 2012,
an award by the National Media Museum and MACK to support the
publication of a book by a previously unpublished photographer.

Thanks to
The National Media Museum
The Wilson Centre for Photography
Kraszna-Krausz Foundation
The John Kobal Foundation
Pierre Brahm

With special thanks to
Michael Mack, Grégoire Pujade-Lauraine, Izabella Scott, Pedro Alfacinha,
Poppy Melzack, Greg Hobson, Polly Fleury, Charlotte Cotton, Leslie Searles,
Martina Bacigalupo, Annalisa d'Angelo, Olga Hoffman, Giorgia Fiorio,
Gabriel Bauret, Benoît Rivero, Rosalba Ruffa, Vanessa Claux, Virginie Chibau,
Emile Loreaux, Anne-Lise Cornet, Pierre Clauss, Chiara Goia, Ali Taptık,
Bohnchang Koo, Mark Midung'a, Mika Sunahachi, Fuki Yamane, Kensuke and
Naoko Miyazaki, Ochi Batdavaajav, Délia Rémy, my family and most of all
my husband Nicoló Giudice.

Printed by optimal media

MACK
25 Denmark Street London WC2H 8NJ
www.mackbooks.co.uk

ISBN 978-1-907946-25-7